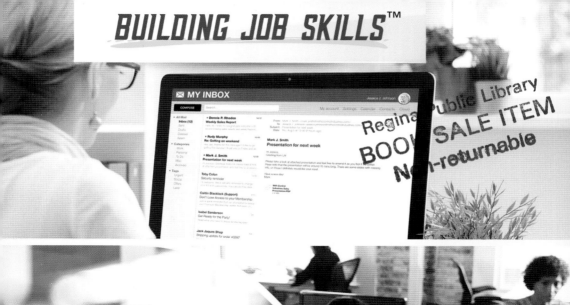

BUILDING JOB SKILLS™

BECOME
A GREAT
COMMUNICATOR
AT WORK

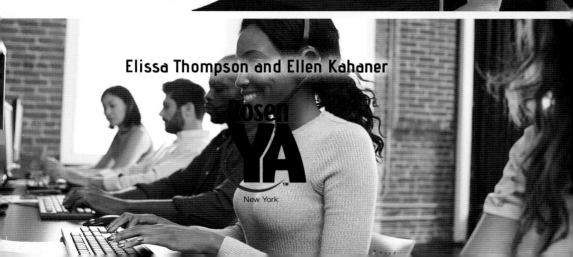

Elissa Thompson and Ellen Kahaner

Rosen
YA™
New York

Published in 2020 by The Rosen Publishing Group, Inc.
29 East 21st Street, New York, NY 10010

Library of Congress Cataloging-in-Publication Data

Names: Thompson, Elissa, author. | Kahaner, Ellen, author.
Title: Become a great communicator at work / Elissa Thompson and Ellen Kahaner.
Description: First edition. | New York : Rosen Publishing, 2020. | Series:
Building job skills | Includes bibliographical references and index.
Identifiers: LCCN 2019013991 | ISBN 9781725347106
(library bound) | ISBN 9781725347090 (pbk.)
Subjects: LCSH: Business communication—Juvenile literature.
| Interpersonal communication—Juvenile literature.
Classification: LCC HF5718 .T4635 2020 | DDC 650.101/4—dc23
LC record available at https://lccn.loc.gov/2019013991

Manufactured in the United States of America

CONTENTS

INTRODUCTION

Can anybody hear me?

As a teen, it can sometimes feel like it's hard to be taken seriously. Your parents have their heads down, answering work email on their phones. Your friends are all busy with their own activities. And your boss—well, your boss has a lot going on, too. But you have a great idea that could really help improve things at work. How do you get your coworkers to pay attention to you and listen, really listen, to what you have to say?

It can sometimes feel impossible to be heard and taken seriously, especially at work where you might be the youngest one there. But it can be done. There are skills you can practice and techniques you can use to communicate effectively at work. From active listening—being heard starts with listening, believe it or not—to interpreting body language, you can learn to tailor your message to the people who most need to hear it.

Remember, as a teen there is so much you have to offer, both to the world at large and at your workplace. You are part of the generation, iGen, born in the mid-1990s or later. That means you grew up with cell phones and the internet as a part of your normal life. That also means you can offer a different perspective, new ideas, and an innate understanding of the world around you. You see things differently than those older

Communicating effectively with others is an important part of succeeding at work—and in life. You have a voice and you deserve to be heard.

than you—and that's a good thing. Your perspective can be super valuable to your boss and coworkers.

Think of climate change activist Greta Thunberg. She is a teenager to whom the whole world listens. It wasn't always this way. "All my life I've been invisible, the invisible girl in the back who doesn't say anything," Thunberg told Somini Sengupta at the *New York Times*. But she began protesting and garnering worldwide attention.

Greta Thunberg is a climate change activist who uses her voice to try and help the world. Here she's speaking for the Belgian Youth for Climate, on February 21, 2019, in Brussels, Belgium.

Greta chooses her words wisely. She told Sengupta, "I only say what's necessary." Greta is so persuasive that she convinced her parents to become vegan, meaning they do not eat or use any animal products, like eggs or milk. Then she persuaded her mother, a famous opera singer who traveled a great deal, to stop flying, because the carbon emissions from airplanes are so detrimental to the atmosphere. This made the whole world pay attention. "It felt very good to be listened to," Greta said.

You too can learn to command attention like Greta. The first step is to begin to pay attention to those around you. Think about how you feel when an adult bosses you around, telling you what to do without stopping to hear your point of view. Your coworkers wouldn't like that if you did that to them either. By considering what you have to say, hearing the perspectives of those around you, and being informed before speaking, you'll be well on your way to effectively communicating at work. By listening, you can be heard!

PHONE DOWN, HEAD UP

T o be a great communicator, first you must learn to listen. By paying attention to what's going on around you, you will be better able to tailor your message to its intended target. The first step? Putting down your phone.

STEP AWAY FROM YOUR PHONE

Your phone can keep you from paying attention to the world around you. You know this. But did you know it can also affect your job? "Smartphones, beeping and buzzing with their alerts and notifications that incoming messages have arrived, interrupt flow, and can decrease productivity," wrote Wendy L. Patrick, PhD, in *Psychology Today*. Patrick wrote about a 2017 study on using smartphones at work. "Smartphones also prompt users to check them frequently, further impacting the ability to engage in consistently productive work." The buzz of notifications in particular can keep you attached to your phone, checking and rechecking,

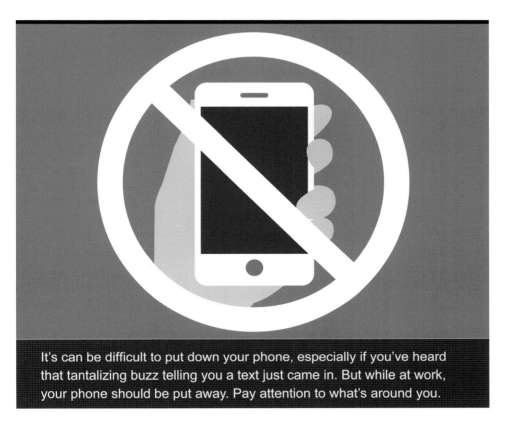

It's can be difficult to put down your phone, especially if you've heard that tantalizing buzz telling you a text just came in. But while at work, your phone should be put away. Pay attention to what's around you.

even if there's nothing new to look at. But when you're at work, you should be paying attention to what's happening around you. So shut off your notifications. If your phone doesn't buzz constantly, you won't be alerted, and you'll be less tempted to pick it up. Try putting your phone away somewhere you can't see it at work.

MANAGING YOUR PHONE

Sure, you love your phone, but taking a break can be a good idea, too. One way to start stepping away from your smart device is to pay attention to how much

PRACTICING MINDFULNESS

One way to help yourself pay attention is to practice mindfulness. What does this mean? Mindfulness is about focusing on your environment without judgment. If you're feeling overwhelmed at work, take a moment to try these practices, as explained by the Mayo Clinic. It can help calm and center you so you're ready to focus at work.

- **Pay attention.** It's hard to slow down and notice things in a busy world. Try to take the time to experience your environment with all of your senses—touch, sound, sight, smell, and taste. For example, when you eat a favorite food, take the time to smell, taste, and truly enjoy it.
- **Live in the moment.** Try to intentionally bring an open, accepting, and discerning attention to everything you do. Find joy in simple pleasures.
- **Accept yourself.** Treat yourself the way you would treat a good friend.
- **Focus on your breathing.** When you have negative thoughts, try to sit down, take a deep breath, and close your eyes. Focus on your breath as it moves in and out of your body. Sitting and breathing for even just a minute can help.

you're using it in the first place. Utilize usage apps to be aware of how many hours a day you're looking at your phone. You might be surprised. A 2018 Pew Research Center study found that 45 percent of teens say they are online "almost constantly." By being aware of how often you spend on your phone, and even how many times you pick it up a day, you can make a more informed decision about taking a step back.

FIRST, OBSERVE

Almost fifty years ago, baseball legend Yogi Berra said, "You can observe a lot by watching." Seeing with a questioning mind is an important part of taking on the responsibility of a job. In science class, you might have conducted experiments where you made observations. You might have asked questions based on what you saw so that you could formulate a hypothesis. Did you test it out and see if it was true? These same skills can apply on the job.

Before Jenny's interview, she used her critical observation skills to collect information and ask herself questions. During the interview she tested out her theory that there were no young workers in the store and found that she was correct. Once she started working, she used her critical observation skills to learn from her mistakes. She noticed the unexpected. All these behaviors showed that she was successfully engaged at work.

Critical observation allows you not only to take information in but also to analyze it and to apply it so that you can make wise choices. Imagine if Jenny had arrived for her interview with no preparation. She might have walked into the interview wearing an inappropriate outfit. Or perhaps she wouldn't have known what she could say to stand out from the other applicants. Being observant and paying attention to details helped Jenny establish a connection of trust with her new employers.

They could tell that she was someone who cared about the business running efficiently and would want to help them achieve that goal.

THE POWER OF PAYING ATTENTION

All businesses have their own customs and style, making up their company culture. Noticing these details will help you to fit in. Pay attention to the following points:

- The dress code. It's often safer to dress up from the norm at your job rather than to dress down. Jenny dressed more conservatively for her job than she did at school, meaning she wore button-down shirts instead of T-shirts, and khakis instead of her usual favorite worn-out jeans. If you wear a uniform at your job, notice who looks the neatest, and ask that person how she or he maintains that appearance.
- Communication style. Observe how other employees deal with customers, coworkers, and the boss. Do people call each other by first names or last names? What are the most common small talk topics? You can use this information to start up your own conversations.
- Rules. Does your starting time at 4:00 p.m. really mean your boss

wants you there at 3:55 p.m.? What gets people in trouble at the job? Use your critical observation skills and ask yourself why these situations happen and how they could be avoided.

- Safety issues. Staying safe on the job is an important concern for everyone. If you see

While you are at work, paying attention pays off. By being mindful of what is happening around you, you can do a great job.

something out of place, report it or fix it. Even a few drops of water spilled on the floor can cause an accident. Don't be a worker who says, "Someone else will take care of it" or "It's not my job."

- The big picture. How does your job fit in to the way your company works? What is your company's mission and direction? Being aware of the larger environment will help you to understand how you fit into it all. You may be able to figure out how to move ahead.

HOW TO OBSERVE

Critical observation is a skill that you can use throughout your life. By closely observing what is happening, you can better react to situations and understand what is happening.

1. Pay attention to body language. What a person says may be different from what his or her body language is saying. Jenny noticed that her interviewer was glancing at his watch although he sounded friendly. She realized she had no time to waste in getting her point across.
2. Take initiative. If you notice something out of the ordinary, don't assume someone else will fix it. Take the initiative and report it to a supervisor or fix it yourself.
3. Ask why. Question what you see. If it's not possible to write things down in the moment, take notes later. Jenny took mental notes

By observing what is happening around you, and listening closely to others, you can learn a lot about your job. This will help you to become a valued employee.

on what she saw when she walked around the shop. These notes helped her formulate questions to ask during her interview.

4. Help others. If you see a coworker having difficulty, lend a hand. Don't do someone else's job, but offer to assist if you can. You will be displaying cooperation and good teamwork behaviors.

5. Admit your mistakes. If you do something wrong, don't try to cover it up. Investigate what happened and try to learn what to do next time. This will show initiative and also help you not to make the same mistake twice.

6. Ask someone. If you are uncertain about what you have observed, check it out with a trusted coworker.

7. Use your senses. All five senses can help you observe. An extreme example of this idea would be if you smell smoke or gas.

Now that you've put down your phone, centered your mind, and analyzed what's happening in your workplace, you're ready to start reading!

MYTHS & FACTS

Myth: People don't really use their smartphones at work.
Fact: A 2018 study from Udemy, an online school, found that millennials and members of iGen say they use their phones for two hours per day at work. That means the average eight-hour work day is cut down to six. To put it another way, if you work a forty-hour week, you could lose at least a full day of productivity. That's time you could be spending figuring out what's going on in your office and furthering your career.

Myth: Smartphones do not affect people's brains.
Fact: Every time something you post to social media gets a like, you get a hit of dopamine. This makes you feel good. That feeling is something your brain begins to want more and more. It's hard to say no to posting more and more and checking more and more— even for adults.

Myth: It's impossible to stop looking at your phone.
Fact: You can do it. One tip to breaking your smartphone habit: engage in something else. Put your focus and attention elsewhere—like the tasks you should be doing at work, or what your boss is saying in that important meeting you're in. By staying engaged with what's happening at work, you can retrain your brain to pay attention to the world around you.

READING UP

All that reading comprehension work you've done in school can pay off big time at work. The information you can gather from reading can help you to become an amazing workplace communicator.

KNOWING WHAT'S UP AT WORK

Dealing with the closing procedures reminded Amanda of her high school English class. No, she wasn't reading a novel, short story, or poem, but the way her boss talked about gathering information from what she read sounded similar to homework assignments she'd completed.

Amanda collected the cheese shakers from the tables, put them into the walk-in refrigerator, shut it tightly, and marked a check next to that task. The strategies that helped her become a better reader in high school would also help her on the job.

Paying attention to what you read is an important part of successful job performance. Imagine if Amanda

You've done reading assignments for school. Reading for work is just as important. So be sure to read that employee manual. It has important information that can help you succeed.

had left the cheese shakers on the table. Or if the refrigerator door wasn't properly closed. The cheese might have gone rancid. The food in the refrigerator could have been spoiled. A big part of working in any industry is carefully following safety procedures so that your health, the health of your coworkers, and the health of those you serve isn't jeopardized. Although you may start at the bottom rung of the ladder, the way you can work your way up—getting promotions and raises—is by performing your job with excellence.

READ, READ, READ

On the job, you can expect to read a variety of material. There are several different strategies you can use to make sure you properly digest all the info you need to do a great job.

WHAT'S THE PURPOSE?

Your purpose for reading, that is, why you are reading and what you want to learn, will influence how you read. You might be getting directions on how to do your job. Maybe you need to become informed about a company policy. Your purpose could be to gain an understanding of an idea or a concept. Keeping your purpose in mind will help you focus on what you need to pull from the text.

Ask these questions to help you determine the best strategies for effective and efficient reading: What is my purpose? How can I prepare to read? Can I retell, visualize, and explain what I just read? Do I need to read to the entire document? How can I use writing to help me understand what I read? A memo or short email can be read quickly. Look for the main idea in the subject line or opening sentence. A manual that gives you directions for doing your job will be read more slowly. You may have to read and reread.

After Amanda was hired, her boss gave her a pamphlet. Before reading it, she thought about her purpose. She was learning background information about the restaurant: its concept and how it was developed. On the job, she read about the closing procedures. Her reading purpose was twofold: to

Think about your purpose for reading before you begin looking over any text. Do you need one small piece of info? Or should you pay close attention to the entire document?

inform herself about specific tasks and to read the special procedures she needed to follow. Her list of tasks included sweeping, taking out garbage, covering all food with plastic wrap, and putting the food in the walk-in refrigerator. She read the special procedure for cleaning the grill.

There are many purposes for reading on the job. Identifying what your purpose is will keep you focused as you read.

PREPARING WITH PRIOR KNOWLEDGE

Preparing to read gets you ready for taking in the content ahead. Remember when you were beginning a new unit in class and the teacher would ask you what you already knew about the subject? She was helping you activate your background or prior knowledge so that you could have an easier time adding new information to what you already know. Why? You have a better chance of understanding and remembering new information if it makes contact with what you already know.

Amanda considered what she already knew about closing procedures from her previous job. She knew that the perishable foods needed to be put in the refrigerator. She knew that the kitchen had to be sparkling clean and ready for start-up the next day. She was ready to find out what the particular details were of this restaurant's closing procedures.

Skimming can also help you prepare to read. Amanda skimmed the list. She took two minutes to quickly read it over. This helped her gain a sense of what she was supposed to accomplish. How many steps were there? How much time did she think this procedure would take? Asking these questions prepared her for the task ahead. She looked over a diagram of the kitchen and the seating chart. She paid attention to any writing that was boldfaced, underlined, or italicized. Skimming gave her an overview of the whole job. Now she was ready to carefully read the first item on the list.

The next time you get a reading assignment in a textbook, practice activating your prior knowledge. You can try skimming on a homework chapter by reading the first sentence of every paragraph (which often contains the main idea).

RETELLING, VISUALIZING, AND EXPLAINING

Three strategies that you can use to test your understanding of what you've read are retelling, visualizing, and explaining.

Retelling or restating is putting what you just read into your own words. When Amanda read that she needed to "secure the refrigerator door," she tried to put that instruction into words she would use in her everyday life. If you're having trouble restating what you read, it may show that you need to look up a word in the dictionary or another reference guide. You might need to ask your coworker or boss a question. Use retelling to see if you understand what you are reading.

Visualizing is when you let the words you are reading make a picture in your mind. While Amanda was reading, she visualized or pictured the procedure. This not only helped her understanding but it also made it easier for her to remember.

FOLLOW THAT SOURCE

To do a great job at work, you might want to do some research about your industry or company on your own time. But it's important to make sure that the sources you are reading are valid and correct. Here are a few tips to make sure that what you are reading is a trusted source.

1. Check the URL. Is the web address a verifiable source, like CNN or the *New York Times*? That's good. Also look at the end of the web address. ".edu" and ".gov" addresses mean the website is being run by a school or government agency, which is a good sign. If the end of the URL looks suspicious, like ".com.co" or similar, you might have a fake site on your hands.
2. Once you click on an article, look it over. Use your critical thinking skills. Is there a publication date listed? That is often a sign that an article is valid. Are there spelling mistakes? That's a sign that the article is fake and should not be trusted.
3. Fact-check. If you read something that seems really wild or too good to be true, you should fact-check it. Take the potentially fake statement in question and do an internet search on it. Does it pop up in other valid places? Or is it perhaps debunked on a site like Snopes?

Learning about your industry and company is a great way to impress at work. But make sure what you're learning is correct to really wow your coworkers.

Explaining is when you tell someone else what you know. Amanda explained the procedure to a coworker, which gave her another chance to work on her understanding.

Be cautious when you search for info online. Use reputable websites. Check the URL and text for any grammatical errors. If something is ubelievable, do an internet search to see if the result comes up elsewhere.

REREADING IS READING

Readers often wonder whether it is necessary to read the whole text. When is it OK to read selectively? It helps to think about your purpose. If you are going to be responsible for knowing the entire task or understanding the big picture, then chances are you need to read every word. Amanda was anxious to start the closing-up procedure. She forced herself to read every word of the closing procedure list. And she was glad she did! The very last item was just as important as the first.

If you're in a hurry or stressed, you may want to jump through the text and read too quickly. Slow down. Give yourself the time to absorb the information. A common phrase in reading classes these days is: reading is rereading. Children are being taught to reread everything they've read to get more meaning out of a text. At a job, rereading can help you catch important information you may have missed the first time.

WRITE TO READ

You can use writing to help you remember and understand what you have read. In high school, important study skills you learned are how to take notes, how to use a highlighter marker, and how to write questions and comments in the margin or in your notebook. All of these strategies can help you on the job. When Amanda was first learning the closing procedures, she wrote down questions about what she didn't understand so that she would remember to ask about them. She used a highlighter to underline the important information so that she would be able to quickly find what she needed. She tested herself by writing down the key points on a separate sheet of paper, and then she cross-checked her list against the actual closing procedures to make sure she would remember them. She was using writing to enhance her reading comprehension.

WHEN IT'S OKAY TO SKIM

If you are just looking for a specific piece of information, you can scan, or glance quickly over, the page for a keyword or phrase. When Amanda needed to recheck the directions for cleaning the blender, she moved her eyes quickly over the page looking for the word "blender." Scanning will help you locate what you need without reading every document from start to finish.

In a wide range of jobs, reading is not optional: it is a requirement. It may be something you do every day on your job or only occasionally. But if you practice these reading strategies, you will become a stronger reader whenever you use this skill.

LISTEN AND LEARN

Listening to others can greatly increase your understanding of a situation. Paying attention can give you important information. Then when you do speak up you will have something of value to say.

STOP, LOOK, AND LISTEN

A good listener is an active listener. Identify your purpose for listening and stay focused. You may be listening to learn how to do a task, get directions, figure out a problem, or gather information. Check your understanding to make sure that you "get it." Listening is a far more complicated process that just hearing something. Listening involves an interaction between you and another person. First you receive a message, then process it, and finally acknowledge that you understood.

On the job, you have to make your best effort to listen and understand what is going on around you. Jonathan thought he heard what the customer had

When your boss or coworker stops by to talk, pay attention. Stop what you are doing, put away your screens, and look him or her in the eye. It feels good to be listened to.

said. She had come in carrying several heavy bags and had looked distracted while she placed her order. He got upset when he handed her the sandwich she had ordered, and she complained that it wasn't what she wanted. They argued and she left without her food. Jonathan didn't make use of "listening" to her body language. If he had taken a moment to repeat the order back to the customer, checking his own understanding, he would have successfully completed the transaction.

Imagine that you are interviewing for a job and you misunderstand a question. The answer you give could sink your prospects. If you use active listening strategies, chances are you will respond appropriately. Some jobs require that you take phone messages. If you mishear, you could cause a big problem for your company. Listening attentively shows that you have the

With active listening, you must pay attention to more than what someone is saying. What is his or her facial expression telling you? His or her body language? These are all clues to a person's true message.

communication skills necessary to navigate the choppy waters of your work environment.

PRACTICING EMPATHY

Empathizing, or putting yourself in someone else's shoes, will help you become a better listener. Jonathan's customer might have been having a bad day for any number of personal reasons—maybe the woman was reprimanded at work, or her child was sick. If he had tried to listen by imagining himself in her situation, he may have been better able to respond in the moment.

ASSUME POSITIVE INTENT

If you get frustrated with a customer or coworker, it can be hard to listen to what he or she has to say. But try to imagine where he or she is coming from. It can make it easier on you as well. "Most people, according to one study, have about 150 undone tasks at any time," says Dr. Amit Sood, the creator of the Mayo Clinic Resilient Mind program. "We're just meeting one deadline after another. Most people are really filled with responsibilities that they have to do. So we should give others a break."

One way to do this is to use a strategy called Assume Positive Intent. It means offering people the benefit of the doubt. Assume your coworkers, customers, and bosses are doing the best they can, just like you. Allow that everyone has problems of his or her own. This can calm your frustrations with a forgetful customer or a slow-moving coworker. Give it a try!

To effectively empathize with someone, don't try to put a positive spin on things. Trying to point out a silver lining, or telling someone that "at least" they don't have another problem is not helpful, says Dr. Brené Brown, a best-selling author and professor at the University of Houston. "If I share something with you that's very difficult, I would rather you say, 'I don't even know what to say right now. I'm just so glad you told me,' " Brown explained in her popular RSA Short YouTube video. "Rarely can a response make something better, what makes something better is connection." So if someone at work is having a bad day, try listening. You could help make a difference.

THE IMPORTANCE OF THINKING OBJECTIVELY

Without even realizing it, your opinions may be causing you to filter out what someone else is saying, especially if you disagree with him or her. Be aware of your own biases. Try to understand what is being said from the speaker's point of view. Listening with an open mind can be one of the most difficult things to do. Listening is key to understanding what someone else needs. By being more sensitive to the speaker, active listening helps you take the appropriate action.

Try these strategies to see if they can help you improve your listening skills:

1. Repeat the information to the speaker to see if you heard it all and accurately.

2. Summarize what you heard to see if you got
 the gist.
3. Restate in your own words or paraphrase to
 process further what you heard and confirm
 that you got it right.
4. Take notes to help you remember.

If you feel overwhelmed when someone is speaking to you, and you are
not sure you will be able to remember all the details, take notes. It can help
with recall later.

5. Politely ask the speaker to repeat something that you didn't hear.
6. Use active listening body language: maintain eye contact, lean forward at the waist, and turn your head toward the speaker.
7. Ask questions to clarify your understanding at pause points in the conversation.
8. Notice how the speaker's delivery makes it easier or more difficult to get the message, and adjust your listening strategies accordingly.
9. Be aware that your environment affects how you listen. If you're in a poorly ventilated room, sitting on an uncomfortable folding chair, with sirens blaring outside the window, your listening skills will be challenged.
10. You may have heard the expression, "It's just business." This is another way of saying don't take what people say personally. In work situations, if you have an emotional response to what someone is saying, try to count to ten, take a deep breath, and use a listening strategy that will help you re-engage.

Learning how to be an active listener takes practice. Listen with purpose. Be aware of what you bring to the situation in terms of prior knowledge and your own point of view. Use strategies to monitor your own comprehension. Understand that listening is complex and requires your full presence and attention.

TALK SO PEOPLE
WILL LISTEN

When communicating at work, you want to make sure you are heard. But how to do it? Talking about work can sometimes feel intimidating. Maybe you are making a cold call to see if there is a job opening or networking with friends and family. You could be going to a job fair or speaking with the school guidance counselor. You might be on your way to a job interview. If you have a job, you will need to talk to your boss about your schedule. You and your coworkers may need to discuss cooperating on tasks. Your project might be overdue, and you will have to explain to your supervisor why you missed the deadline. At some point, you will probably have to call in to your job because you're sick or you're going to be late. Using inappropriate speech can cause you problems on the job. But there are certain tools that can help you speak with confidence and be heard.

HOW TO BE HEARD

When you speak, you want to be understood. Although you can't always predict how someone will respond, the chances of the communication going well are much greater if you speak clearly and with confidence. On the job, this is particularly important. What if Evan returned from the post office, and in a panic, blurted out to his boss that he forgot to put the return addresses on the envelopes? His boss would not only be angry but would also resent that he is left to fix the problem. What if Evan said he was sorry using the same tone of voice he might use with a friend? His boss might feel as if Evan's apology was insincere or that he wasn't taking responsibility for his mistake. Evan had to prepare before he spoke to his boss. A situation that could lead to his termination might actually turn in his favor. A lot was riding on his effective use of speech.

SPEAK UP!

When you were a young child, a parent may have said "use your inside voice" when you were talking too loudly in a restaurant or other public place. It was good advice because it was teaching you about using the appropriate volume for a particular situation. When you are on the job, your delivery or how you say your words is as important as the words themselves. Make the appropriate choices by considering all the aspects of your voice.

Whether you are answering questions in an interview or addressing a serious problem with your

Voicing your thoughts at work can be a great idea. But first, prepare what you want to say, and think about what you want to accomplish. Then go for it!

boss, it is necessary to speak up in the work world. Having a strategy will help you rise to the occasion. Remembering and implementing the Three Ps can help make it easier for you to speak during work-related situations: preparation, practice, and presence.

PREPARATION

Preparing before you speak will make you less nervous. Ask yourself the following five questions:

- Who is your audience? Your audience is who you will be speaking to. Evan knew that when he explained his mistake to his boss, he would use a different tone of voice than when he talked to his friends. The words he chose showed that he had given careful thought to the situation. He had to make it clear that he was aware of his audience.
- What is your purpose? Evan thought about his purpose. Did his words need to persuade, inform, inspire, or do all of these things? Evan's purpose was to inform his boss of his mistake, and at the same time, persuade him that Evan could use his problem-solving skills to fix the situation. Keeping your purpose in mind will prevent you from drifting off the subject.
- How do you organize what you want to say? Sometimes it is helpful if you can organize what you want to say by jotting down your thoughts first, without worrying about the

order. Then you can try plugging your ideas into an outline or a list of bullet points to help you see a possible organization and whether or not you need more concrete information for support. Evan filled in a simple outline with the following headings: problem and solution.

- What are your main points? Consider what is most important for your audience to know— these are your main points. Evan wanted his boss to know the facts: that he forgot to put the return address on the envelopes. He also wanted his boss to know that he could remedy the situation. He called the post office and asked them to hold the envelopes. He could return to the post office to address the letters. He would put in extra hours to make up for lost time. These are the main points he wanted to make, and they would carry a lot more weight than merely saying "I'm sorry" over and over again.
- What is your objective? Your objective is the action you want your audience to take as a result of listening to you. Evan wanted his boss to give him permission to return to the post office, to accept his offer to make up the time, and to see him as a competent employee.

TEEN ACTIVISM

Today, teens are doing more to try and change the world. Teens like climate change activist Greta Thunberg and gun control activist Emma González are working to make change happen. González survived the school shooting at Marjory Stoneman Douglas High School and became part of a movement to change gun laws. On March 24, 2018, at the March for Our Lives rally in Washington, DC, González spoke in front of tens of thousands of people. After she addressed the crowd, she remained silent several minutes. "Since the time that I came out here, it has been six minutes and 20 seconds," Gonález said. "The shooter has ceased shooting, and will soon abandon his rifle, blend in with the students as they escape, and walk free for an hour before arrest. Fight for your lives, before it's someone else's job." Then she walked off stage. By communicating effectively, Gonzalez was able to inspire a huge group of people to affect change. You, too, have the ability to change the world. You can use your voice to do it.

Gun control advocate Emma González uses her voice to create change at the March For Our Lives on March 24, 2018, in Washington, DC.

PRACTICE

Practicing or rehearsing what you want to say will give you the opportunity to build up your confidence. Evan had only a few moments to practice what he was going to say to his boss, but he knew it was better than going in cold. He glanced at his notes and thought about his audience and purpose. Although he was nervous, he took a deep breath and unclenched his hands. He said his words aloud. He realized that at the end of his apology, he wanted to thank his boss for listening. By practicing, he was able to revise his words. Whether you have a few minutes or a few days to practice, it's important to "rehearse" the words. It will make you more comfortable and give you more confidence for the real thing.

PRESENCE

The way that you project yourself—your presence—determines whether or not you get the attention and respect of your audience. Practicing your presence will help, but you will also need to be alert and focused during your talk. Keep in mind, too, that communication includes your body language and the sound and pace of your voice. Body language refers to communication without words by using your body. The gestures, movements, and mannerisms that you make can be interpreted unconsciously by others as expressions of certain feelings. What you do with your hands, eyes, and feet can speak louder than anything you actually say. If you fiddle with a pencil, shift your eyes back and forth, and tap your foot, your body language will

If you are giving a presentation at work, take a deep breath before speaking. Consider holding a pen in your hand to keep from fidgeting.

distract your audience and convey that you're anxious. Establish good posture, feet solidly planted on the ground, and steady eye contact. Smile, if appropriate. When you are greeting someone, a firm handshake will communicate confidence. In addition, your voice, from its tempo to its tone, influences whether or not you come across as being professional and poised. If you rush and use a disrespectful tone of voice, you will not be taken seriously.

STRIKE A POSE

Whether you are a hair stylist, bank teller, or data entry clerk—in every job, there will come a time when you will need to speak up. Whether it's changing your schedule, asking for a day off, or negotiating a raise, your skill as a speaker will affect the outcome of the communication.

Remember that your delivery is as important as the words that you use. Think of your audience and your purpose. Prepare, practice, and be aware of your presence. Learn from your experiences. These tips will help you for the next time as you develop into an effective speaker on the job.

10 GREAT QUESTIONS
TO ASK A PUBLIC SPEAKER

1. What's the most effective way to get your point across?
2. What is the one thing you do to stay calm before speaking publicly?
3. Do you memorize your speech or just go by broader bullet points?
4. How do you get your audience's attention?
5. What advice would you have for someone who has a fear of public speaking?
6. Do you ever get intimidated by your audience?
7. What's your best tip about giving a successful presentation?
8. What's one thing someone should never do when presenting?
9. What's the one question you wished people asked you about public speaking?
10. What do you do if you can tell the audience isn't listening?

THE POWER OF THE PEN

Communicating via the written word can be powerful and effective. You have time to think of what you want to say and the ability to edit before you send your words along to anyone.

PROFESSIONAL WRITING

Writing that is clear and accurate is a key part of many jobs. Imagine if Isabel wrote down the incorrect information in a phone message. Her boss could have lost out on an opportunity for the company. What if she wrote up the meeting notes or a memo in a way that was confusing or, even worse, misrepresented what people had said? If she kept the schedule disorganized, appointments would be missed and time would be wasted. She had to return emails, answering the questions of potential clients or they might take their business elsewhere. She kept a written record of what she accomplished and what needed to get done

Got writer's block? It can help to write out a first draft longhand, with pen and paper. This may help to get the ideas flowing.

in the future. Her job performance depended on her writing skills.

GETTING BETTER: A STEP-BY-STEP GUIDE TO CLEAR WRITING AT WORK

So how do you make sure your writing is clear and communicates the message you want? There are some steps you can take to make sure your writing is effective. The process begins by determining your audience and purpose. You then work on an organizational plan. Next you choose the information you need. You think about your format. After that, you write your first draft. You revise your writing to make it even better. Finally, you proofread and submit your work.

DETERMINE YOUR AUDIENCE AND PURPOSE

First, you need to determine who your audience is. The audience for your writing is the reader. Sometimes you will be writing to more than one person, and your audience will be wider. Sometimes you will just be writing for yourself. It is important to identify who your audience is because it will influence what you write and the way that you write it. If Isabel is writing a memo to coworkers, she will use a different tone from the one she uses to write to a prospective client. The tone is the sound and attitude of the words. She might use a friendly voice with coworkers and a more formal voice with clients. She might write a few short sentences in an email because her coworkers already know a lot about the company, whereas a potential client will need more detail. When she writes notes for herself, as long as she can read them, that's all that matters. Considering your audience will help you write in the appropriate tone with the appropriate focus.

You also need to establish a purpose for your writing. Your purpose is the reason why you are writing. There are many reasons that you write on the job. Isabel wrote an email to her boss, requesting a day off. Maybe you are sending a calendar invite to coworkers for an important meeting. Isabel often writes business emails to convince people to buy a product. Asking yourself what action you want your audience to take as a result of reading what you have written will help you identify your purpose. Identifying your purpose will keep your writing on the right track.

OUTLINE AN ORGANIZATIONAL PLAN

Organization is key to presenting your thoughts clearly and logically. Consider writing out a short outline, addressing the main points you want to address. Some key bullet points can also focus you as you prepare to write.

Sometimes the amount of information you have to work with in writing is overwhelming. You may wonder

Feeling overwhelmed with everything you have to do? Write out a checklist and tackle items one by one.

what to include and what to leave out. It might help you to use a tip from journalists. Reporters pack a lot of information into the first sentence, or "lede," so that the reader will quickly get the main point and supporting detail. The reader comes away with answers to the Five Ws and H: Who? What? When? Where? Why? And How? Ask yourself if the information you are including is important. Does it help your reader understand your main point by answering the Five Ws and H? If the information you have included is off topic, chances are, you can omit it.

SELECT A FORMAT

The format you choose for your writing will depend on its purpose and audience. Is it a casual email, sales pitch, report, form, or list? The appropriate format will convey to your audience that you understand the conventions of written communication. Ask your boss or coworkers if you can see writing samples that have been used in the past. Isabel, for example, keeps a folder of writing samples on her desk for reference.

TIME TO DRAFT

Not all writing on the job will require that you write a draft first. But if your writing will be read by others, writing a draft can help you communicate more effectively. A draft contains the beginning, middle, and end of what you are writing—the whole piece. A first draft is your first attempt. You can use your outline or bullet points to help you get started. Sometimes you can write one draft and that will work, but often, you will

THE IMPORTANCE OF GRAMMAR

Using correct grammar will make your writing sound professional. Here are some quick tips to make sure your work writing is up to par.

- Do not use slang. If writing an email, start with a "Hello," not "Hey." No emojis or abbreviations like BRB or LOL. You are not shooting a quick text to your friend; you are writing a work email to your boss.
- Don't mix up your homophones. You've learned them in school, and now it's important to keep them straight at work. Remember the differences between "you're/your," "there/their/they're," "its/it's," "two/to/too," and "then/than."
- Watch your punctuation. When you read over your work, make sure every sentence ends with a period. Make sure your commas are consistent, too. If you are using a serial comma—the comma before "and" or "or" before the final item in a list—do so throughout your text.

need to write multiple drafts, adding information, taking out unnecessary detail, and refining your language, to accomplish your purpose. Many writers often say, "writing is rewriting."

You want your writing to be understood. Asking yourself questions can help you revise or change what you have written. Is the main point clear? Will your audience know what you want them to do? Does the organization of the information make sense? Is the tone appropriate for the occasion? Is the language too formal? Too slangy? Have you used too much jargon? Have you indicated if you want a reply? Did you state what date you need the reply by? It can help to read your draft aloud to a coworker or to yourself. It is possible to hear your own errors. A coworker can tell

Before you send out an important document, it is important to proofread. If you can, have a friend or parent read it over, too. He or she might see errors you missed.

you what is confusing. Then you will need to make the necessary changes before considering a draft final.

PROOFREAD

Before you hit Send, you will need to proofread your writing for spelling and grammatical errors. You can use

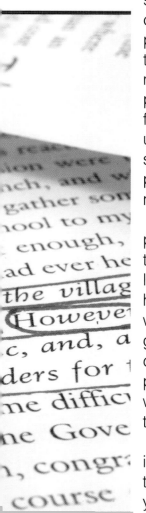

spell and grammar check, although you can't rely on these alone, as they will not pick up on your meaning or tone. You can try a proofreading method that is used by many newspapers and book publishers: print out a hard copy and read it aloud, following along by using your finger to point under each word. This will help you catch small errors and typos. You can make a positive impression if you submit a clean, neat final draft.

Whether writing is a big or small part of your job, you will be expected to communicate clearly through written language. Trying to think about what you have to say, organize it, find the right words, spell correctly, and use proper grammar all at the same time can be daunting. But if you break down the process and take it one step at a time, writing can be less overwhelming on the job.

Communicating clearly at work is an important life skill that will serve you well through your entire career. By putting down your phone and paying attention, you

By working on your communication skills, you can wow everyone at work. Pay attention and think before you speak, and you will find success.

will learn a great deal about your work environment and coworkers. Then when you have something to say or a report to write, you will be able wow your boss, coworkers, and customers with your savvy communication skills.

application The form upon which a statement of one's qualifications for employment are written.

background What you already know that you bring to understanding something new.

body language The signals that your body sends about what you are thinking and feeling; gestures, mannerisms, and movements that one makes while speaking.

company culture The climate of your place of business—including how things are done and the way people dress, talk, and behave.

critical observation Actively thinking and evaluating what you are observing.

debunk To reveal a trick or lie.

homophones Words that sound alike but have different meanings or spellings.

hypothesis An explanation for an observation or problem that is unproven until further investigation and testing.

interview A face-to-face meeting in which an employer formally evaluates the qualifications of a prospective employee for a particular job.

jargon Language that is too technical or specialized to be widely understood outside of a given field.

mannerisms A gesture or habit, often unconscious, sometimes exaggerated.

memo A short, written message that begins with the headings To, From, Date, Subject.

mindfulness The state of total awareness.

networking Meeting new people and exchanging information that helps to further one's career.

point of view The perspective or position from which someone views the world. Being aware of a point of view, including your own, helps you to evaluate the accuracy and usefulness of information.

promotion An advancement in rank or responsibility, often coming with a pay increase.

purpose Your aim or goal.

scan To look for specific information in a text.

serial comma A comma separating the next-to-last item from the final item in a list, preceding "and" or "or."

skim To preview by glancing quickly over the whole text.

small talk Safe topics, such as the weather or holiday plans, to talk about with your coworkers and boss.

unconscious Not conscious, not knowing or aware.

URL Internet address.

Canadian Communication Association
275 Bank Street
Suite 300
Ottawa, Ontario
K2P 2L6
(613) 238-6112 extension 320
Website: http://acc-cca.ca
Email: congress@ideas-idees.ca
Facebook & Twitter: @CCA_ACdC
A bilingual association founded in 1980 for teachers
and professionals to discuss communications
research in Canada.

Do Something
19 West 21st Street
8th Floor
New York, NY 10010
(212) 254-2390
Website: http://www.dosomething.org/us
Facebook, Twitter & Instagram: @dosomething
Teens can volunteer for a wide variety of issues and social
change campaigns via this worldwide organization.

JFF (Jobs for the Future)
88 Broad Street
8th Floor
Boston, MA 02110
(617) 728-4446
Website: http://www.jff.org
Twitter: @jfftweets
Facebook & Instagram: @jobsforthefuture

JFF works to level the playing field so that education and career growth can lead to economic advancement for everyone.

Service Canada
Website: http://www.servicecanada.gc.ca
This Canadian agency provides information about career opportunities, career planning, résumé writing, and job interviewing techniques.

SkillsUSA
PO Box 3000
Leesburg, VA 20177-0300
(703) 777-8810
Website: http://www.skillsusa.org
Facebook, Twitter & Instagram: @SkillsUSA
SkillsUSA is a national nonprofit organization that serves teachers, high school students, and college students who are preparing for jobs in trade, technical, and skilled services, including the health field.

Youth Communication
242 W. 38th Street
6th Floor
New York, NY 10018
Phone: (212) 279-0708
Website: http://youthcomm.org
Facebook & Twitter: @youthcomm
Instagram: @youthcommunication
A program to assist teens, and those who teach them, with writing and building social and emotional skills.

Carroll, Jamuna. *Thinking Critically: Social Networking*. San Diego, CA: ReferencePoint Press, 2018.

Duffy, Claire. *The Teen's Guide to Debating and Public Speaking*. Toronto, Ontario, Canada: Dundurn, 2018.

Gordon, Sherri M. *How to Create Digital Portfolios to Develop Communication Skills*. New York, NY: Rosen Publishing, 2018.

Gosman, Gillian. *Send It: Writing Different Kinds of Emails*. New York, NY: PowerKids Press, 2015.

Hopkins, Lee B., and Serge Bloch. *A Bunch of Punctuation*. Honesdale, PA: WordSong, an imprint of Highlights, 2018.

Hyde, Natalie. *What Is Entrepreneurship?* New York, New York, NY: Crabtree Publishing, 2017.

Koya, Lena, and Heather M. Niver. *Networking Women: Building Social and Professional Connections*. New York, NY: Rosen Publishing, 2018.

Spilsbury, Louise. *Tips for Better Public Speaking*. London: Wayland, 2017.

Suen, Anastasia. *Communicating in the Digital World*. New York, NY: Crabtree Publishing, 2018.

Uhl, Xina M. *Strengthening Collaborative Project Skills*. New York, NY: Rosen Publishing, 2018.

Anderson, Monica, and JingJing Jiang. "Teens, Social Media & Technology 2018." Pew Research Center. May 31, 2018. https://www.pewinternet.org/2018/05/31/teens-social-media-technology-2018.

Bowman, Judith. *Don't Take the Last Donut: New Rules of Business Etiquette*. Franklin Lakes, NJ: Career Press, 2007.

Bruzzese, Anita. *45 Things You Do That Drive Your Boss Crazy and How to Avoid Them*. New York, NY: Penguin Group, 2007.

Jenkins, Ryan. "How to Reduce Smartphone Distraction at Work (and Home)." *Inc.* November 12, 2018. https://www.inc.com/ryan-jenkins/how-to-reduce-smartphone-distraction-at-work-and-home.html.

Laffey, Kelly. "Master These 7 Grammar Tips if You Want to Sound Smarter." Business Insider, May 9, 2018. https://www.businessinsider.com/grammar-tips-and-tricks-for-email-2018-3.

Lawson, Ken. *Successful Communication*. Hauppauge, NY: Barron's, 2006.

Lucero, Louis. "What Emma González Said Without Words at the March for Our Lives Rally." *New York Times.* March 24, 2018. https://www.nytimes.com/2018/03/24/us/emma-gonzalez-march-for-our-lives.html.

Mayo Clinic, "Mayo Clinic Minute: Assume Positive Intent," YouTube, December 28, 2015, https://www.youtube.com/watch?v=yDIXardWUAk.

Mayo Clinic Staff. "Mindfulness Exercises." Mayo Clinic, August 17, 2018. https://www.mayoclinic.org/healthy-lifestyle/consumer-health/in-depth/mindfulness-exercises/art-20046356.

Monarth, Harrison, and Larina Kase. *Confident Speaker*. New York, NY: McGraw Hill, 2007.

Patrick, Wendy L. "How Your Cell Phone Habits Impact Your Productivity." *Psychology Today*, July 30, 2018. https://www.psychologytoday.com/us/blog/why-bad -looks-good/201807/how-your-cell-phone-habits -impact-your-productivity.

Peters, Jennifer. *You're Being Duped: Fake News on Social Media*. New York, NY: Enslow, 2019.

Piphen, Mary. *Writing to Change the World*. New York, NY: Penguin Group, 2006.

The RSA, "Brené Brown on Empathy," YouTube, December 10, 2013. https://www.youtube.com /watch?v=1Evwgu369Jw.

Sengupta, Somini. "Becoming Greta: 'Invisible Girl' to Global Climate Activist, With Bumps Along the Way." *New York Times*, February 18, 2019. https://www .nytimes.com/2019/02/18/climate/greta-thunburg .html?module=inline.

Shapiro, Fred R., ed. *The Yale Book of Quotations*. New Haven, CT: Yale University Press, 2006.

Udemy for Business. "Udemy In Depth: 2018 Work Distraction Report." February 2018. https://research .udemy.com/wp-content/uploads/2018/03/FINAL -Udemy_2018_Workplace_Distraction_Report.pdf.

Vacca, Jo Anne L., Richard T. Vacca, Mary K. Gove, Linda C. Burkey, Lisa A. Lenhart, and Christine A. McKeon. *Reading and Learning to Read*, 6th ed. Boston, MA: Allyn & Bacon, 2006.

Wolfinger, Anne. *Best Career and Education Web Sites: A Quick Guide to Online Job Search, 5th ed.* Indianapolis, IN: Jist Works: 2007.

INDEX

ABOUT THE AUTHORS

Elissa Thompson is a journalist who has been published in *USA Weekend*, the *Baltimore Sun*, and *In Touch Weekly*, among others. She received her master's in journalism from the University of Maryland. She has written and edited several other books for Rosen Publishing. The written word is her preferred method of communication.

Ellen Kahaner earned a master of fine arts degree in writing from Columbia University and a master's degree in the science of teaching from New School University. She is a licensed reading teacher in New York and New Jersey and has had a long career teaching reading and writing. She lives in South Orange, New Jersey, with her husband, Jeremy, and daughter, Sylvia.

PHOTO CREDITS